100 Secrets of the Illuminati for Life Success

The Art of the Highly Effective Badass

The Path to Extreme Illumination and the Secret Rules of Crushing It

By Counselor George Mentz, JD, MBA, CILS

The international award-winning Author of *Quantum Bliss*, host of the American's Wealth Management Law program, international attorney, global educator, and philanthropist delivers an uplifting and motivational combination of analysis about super rich and super successful people to deliver the SECRETS OF HEALTH WEALTH AND SUCCESS.

Understanding the Success Mindset of a Billionaire or True Leader

What Every Leader and Entrepreneur Should Know about Success

Contents

Preface

If you've ever read any self-help books, you'll know that many of them are quite the same. They talk about dealing with people, leading, managing, making money, making good decisions, building things, and cultivating the type of attitude that is necessary to have for success, among other things.

So, there's a lot of common denominators in self-help books. If you read a top success book, however, they're a little bit different – a little bit more straightforward, a little bit more of the WEALTH mindset built into them, which is a no-nonsense, honest approach designed to maximize the reader's time. These books just want to give you the facts and the information needed to get the job done.

This little summary covers a number of key topics, ideas, and concepts that will help you get into the mind of leaders like Trump, Pickens, Gates, Bezos, Google's Page, and other billionaire entrepreneurs. I am not a profiler, but you could call me a scientist of behavioral leadership and metaphysics.

Mind you, I've read hundreds of books written by success gurus, world leaders, and billionaires, and, based on these observations, here are some of the fundamentals that make up the character of someone who makes it BIG. With the information in this book, you will be informed of how top performers think and, more importantly, how a self-made billionaire views you and your ethics.

Don't forget that top leaders have been making billions for 20+ years and have been paying and leading thousands of employees for decades. They have been working tirelessly for decades to become the best they can be, improve their community, be a master builder and philanthropist, and defend his nation: thus, success is NO accident.

This work was originally commissioned at the request of George Mentz at the conclusion of a 25-year research project based upon conversations of over 500 global leaders in over 50 countries, including such self-made giants as CEOs, inventors, MVP Athletes, world champions, presidents, bishops, kings, royalty, billionaires, and top gurus on the subject.

The Law of Achievement was first delivered as a lecture, and part of this famous guidance was given in China, Arabia, Europe, India, Latin America, the West Indies, and throughout Asia.

To go to the next level, read this book intently, contemplate the timeless wisdom contained, take action, and become a master of your destiny. This is the timeless framework for achievement and progress that has been proven to work over the last 25 years.

"Belief is the energy that animates the wings of the soul."
GM

The Process of Manifesting Your Desires

To be successful, one of the first and most important steps is knowing how to manifest your desires into reality. This process is worth the effort to see your dreams come to fruition. Following the steps below, and using the tools outlined in the following sections, you can realize your dreams and become the successful person you wish to become.

1. Our most important quest must begin within ourselves with an esoteric inner enhancement that connects us to the power, creativity, and wisdom of the universe. The inner transformation must be won before looking to external fixes.

2. Consciousness has evolved instinctively through to modern day. Now, we have a choice to make an intelligent, individual mental evolution.

3. There is One Power, and that power can be tapped into if we have a desire for an efficient mind and conscious harmonious connection with the Spirit of the Universe.

4. The Deeper Mind and Authentic Consciousness have the ability to: master imagination, receive intelligent inspiration and intuition, and even develop types of

prescience or psychic powers that allow for a higher order of deductive reasoning, thought, and action.

5. The practice of the presence of God is getting ourselves into the consciousness of our oneness and a harmony with God or the Universal Life Force.

6. The true teaching of the Master was the divine possibility of human potential. "Be ye perfect."

7. Practical metaphysics says that you can have anything you earnestly desire, as we cannot really desire anything that is not already within us seeking expression.

8. Our potential arises from an intuitive awareness of our inner potential, which is a knowingness with an open heart and mind.

9. We can learn the power of willingness to impress ideas and beliefs upon our subconscious minds and to take action.

10. The key is taking responsibility for our thoughts, which are enhanced as a result of our attitudes and feelings.

11. We must work to awaken the mind and allow mindfulness.

12. To have clarity and mental power, we must remain strong and pure of mind. Each day should be analyzed to enhance productivity. Each destructive habit can be

examined and pruned. Distractive thinking should be set aside. The highest meaning and lessons of past events should be cultivated and respected. A healthy respect for the destructive power of certain people, places, and things should be honored.

13.   Robert Frost wrote, "First thing I do in the morning is make up my bed, then I make up my mind."

14.   Words, attitudes, and beliefs are an important part of programming your past, present, and future. "For by thy words thou shalt be justified, and by thy words thou shalt be condemned." (Matthew 12:36-37).

15.   How do I want things to be? Who do I want to be? What do I need to be to become the ideal?

16.   The first step is to construct a mental prototype, archetypal idea, or the mental equivalent. If the imagination is practiced, the deeper mind will work around the clock, twenty-four hours a day, to assist you in your objectives in conjunction with your impression of the creative life force.

17.   <u>Affirmations</u> have power because they are decreed from a spiritual consciousness. From the work we can speak with confidence, constructiveness, and harmony with

the universe. The law is set in motion with the word and written word.

18. We must prepare ourselves mentally each day. Each mental seed will bring forth after its kind, feeling, and intention.

19. Visualizations have power when developed with a spiritual intent and feeling. Any desired result projected on the mental picture screen of your inner mind will become an emblazoned potentiality.

20. Judge Troward emphasized the power of deep and heartfelt feeling when engaging decrees, affirmations, imagination, and visualization. Know with calm aspiration that all conditions and substance are available for the manifestation of your ideals.

21. Inspiration is created by the WILL and willingness to receive it. When we are open to the spirit, then vivifying thoughts, ideas, and feelings will flow into us.

22. Meet the Spirit of the Universe halfway with your mind, thoughts, ideas, and actions.

23. Know with constructive awareness that the beneficent abundant universe will present opportunity and solutions for you to act upon the completion of your objectives.

24. From this day forward, practice mental constructive thinking. Become determined to think and speak in a way that builds your character, beliefs, and reality.

25. When the mind is made up, it continues to exercise creative power and sets to work out the purpose of that intention and focus.

26. Spirit and substance work together: Substance supplies something from which a selection can be made and action can be imparted where the manifestation of our future is an expression of the spirit.

27. Take action on your ideas and the inspiration provided to you to complete your daily tasks and obligations that lead to your purpose and fulfillment.

28. The spirit creates through self-contemplation. What you contemplate as the law of your being becomes your reality.

29. Faith is the substance of things unseen. Faith is focused energy. Applied faith is a bit of constructive energy instilled into a belief or an idea, or even a healing. When all things are in balance, an extra bit of faith can stack the energy and potentialities in your favor.

30.   If you are determined to utilize your will to make yourself sicker, you can achieve this, but in the same vein, you may use your will and determination to become more healthy, vibrant, enthusiastic, aware, and mindful.

31.   A pure harmonious relationship with the universe is what allows for a cosmic metaphysical marriage. This unification can allow anyone to become a master of their destiny.

32.   We cultivate the consciousness of oneness with God. To do this, we engage in contemplation or prayer, which is the consciousness of life. Contemplative prayer is a systematic, scientific way of expanding our thoughts and getting in tune with the universal flow of energy. "Be still and know that I am" (Psalms 46:10) and in that stillness, listen.

33.   To cultivate an idea, objective or desire into true purpose, we must be receptive and have a WILLINGNESS to achieve it. Our will assists in rightly molding the faculty of imagination.

34.   The subconscious reasons deductively. Our manifest life is a process of becoming, and we can evolve into new excellence or creativity each day.

35.   Consciousness is a generator that provides the degree of love, joy, and peace we radiate into ourselves and outward.

36.   While there are many ingredients to the recipes of harmony or prayer, gratitude is a key term as it dispels discouragement and allows for a living faith, flow, and effective consciousness.

37.   Your mental and spiritual consciousness will determine your world view, which in turn will dramatically affect your experience and journey. Thus, the totality of your daily thoughts, thinking, actions, and omissions IS the quality of your consciousness.

38.   Action and work must be in the here and now, and they must be engaged with focus and contemplativeness, not with anxious thought. If we believe in our purpose and objectives, it will energize our actions and thoughts.

39.   Each day is an opportunity to take steps in the direction of the desired ideals, higher consciousness, harmony, and higher order.

The 100 Laws of the Illuminated Master

The Illuminated Master is an expert at tapping the power of the mind to become the best version of yourself, which will translate to success. Pay attention to these lessons, as they are invaluable when implemented and ingrained in your daily life.

1. Being Well-Read – The Guru Bookshelf

First of all, it seems many leaders and billionaires are well-read, stay sharp, and maintain a bit of healthy paranoia. They seem to be the type of people to stay very, very informed and to dedicate time every day to catching up on the news and debriefing on different current issues, whether it's in the press or media, radio, or television. They also seem to want to talk to a lot of people so they can keep their fingers on the pulse of their business, humanity, and society, because they are very interested in their people and the success of their companies, as well as the success of their customers worldwide.

Many of the common themes in books by billionaires are about leading, surrounding yourself with good people, serving your customers and knowing your audience, and not being an average person—to be great. With every particular goal, objective, or task, we do have to know who our customer is, what they might want, who the target buyer is, and how to build something that's authentic or having value, not just cheap junk. Further, he is a master of how to appeal to the people (the masses) and to influencers, and how to stick to our convictions and perseverance. Billionaires and leaders tend to read the works of philosophers, religious leaders, legendary figures, and history books of varying kinds, including works by Von Goethe, Buddha, Schopenhauer, Kant, Aristotle, Pythagoras, Marcus Aurelius, Ben Franklin, Swedenborg, Confucius, Sun Tzu, and many more.

2. The Analytical Mind of a Supercharged Billionaire and Leader

The first thing you want to do is to try and get into the mind of the world leader. Obviously, they have learned different methods of analytical reasoning over their lifetimes, so they talk a little bit about strategies like multi-faceted focusing or multilevel thinking, which really is just about using both the left and right sides of your brain. You hear about people who are able to drive subconsciously, essentially using their mind to drive their car without really thinking about it whether it's a stick shift or an automatic, and then there's the other part of the mind that might be talking on the phone. What those people are getting at is that using both sides of the mind, the conscious and the subconscious, or the mind and the memory to make logical and intuitive decisions simultaneously. But, many of us know that this is a developed skill when it comes to being a master builder.

3. Being Bold and Authentic

Top selling books on human potential talk about staying true to yourself, being authentic, standing up for your constructive beliefs, and being purposeful and bold. Many American writers show hints of Ralph Waldo Emerson and von Goethe in their writings. They seem to have been influenced quite a bit by being authentic and truthful and bold and purposeful.

4. Good Routines Good Information

In twenty-first century billionaires' writings, the most successful people practice great routines, stay informed, read different literature from multiple sources, and seek out different viewpoints. They also use metaphorical thinking in terms of pictures, ideas, and words and creating solutions using visualization. That means cultivating great ideas, visualizing great plans, and then restructuring problems to make them broader in a sense. Essentially, that's just looking at problems from different angles and different views and seeing how something would work if you changed a few variables. This is a very architectural and special view that most engineers and scientists would have. But, the analytical skill related to this view requires knowledge, skill, experience, and a bit of genius.

5. Staying Ahead in the Game of Life

Supercharged people talk about being prepared for all of your potential customers, including voters or buyers, and they also talk about staying a few steps ahead of the competition.

You're trying to visualize or understand a few moves ahead of the players in the chess game, as they say, specifically knowing that if you do one move, then what will the other person do? That type of forward thinking can propel you into success.

6. Get Your Mind Right – Focus and Confidence

Winners also want people around them to have a focused, confident mind – a mind that is not a "house divided against itself." Many successful folks use self-affirmation or auto-suggestion and recommend telling yourself that you are brilliant and that you have creative genius. Test it out for yourself by just seeing if this type of internal statement changes your mindset. You'll discover that you are more open minded to see future potential in the ups and downs of the world. This is not a delusional tactic but rather a tactic to build your mind and analytical thinking skills so you do not limit yourself.

7. Know the Rules, Play Fair, and Win with a Positive Mindset

Great business people talk generously about playing fair and trying to be a decent person with integrity and treating others like you want to be treated. However, these same superstars say you have to keep a strong shield up and protect yourself, your energy, and your positive wavelength or mindset. Don't let other people's static, bitterness, or just distractions take you off of your game, because to win, you've got to stay in control. When you encounter negativity, don't take other people personally. Most of the time it's just business or, like any sporting match, it's about winning under the rules at hand.

8. Boldness with Humility

In many bestselling success books, the whole theme is about getting out of your comfort zone, going the extra mile, taking healthy risks, and encouraging us to not take ourselves too seriously. In fact, quite a bit of literature out there says you shouldn't take yourself too seriously, that you have to keep one foot in reality and the other in humility while staying focused on determination, persistence, and sincerity. But consciously, we must maintain enough humility to keep our eyes open and stay aware of what's going on around us.

9. Capitalize on Your Assets and Skills

Top performers consistently talk about capitalizing on your skills, efforts, and successes. You need to capitalize on where your best talents can be maximized and continuously improve what you achieve, whether it's in business, family, your personal or athletic life, etc. Avoid complacency!

That doesn't mean to just stay paranoid; it means staying fit spiritually, physically, and bodily. Then, you're better able to maintain your productivity levels and your enthusiasm. On top of that, sometimes you just have to stop and take a moment in life and look at what's out there and just say, "Hey, it's a beautiful world. It's a beneficent universe. Good things can happen."

10. Beat to Your Own Drum

You just can't spend your whole life keeping up with the Joneses, and you need to dance to the beat of your own drum, keep your own momentum, and learn to get into your own zone and be who you're supposed to be. Try to respond to life according to who you are, authentically. Work hard, but allow things to come naturally with synchronicity.

11.   Stay Sharp and Agile

We all have times when we need to RE-TOOL and re-motivate ourselves for success, but the key is really just to stay on track, keep moving, and don't let things slip through your fingers. Don't get lazy!

12.   Know Thyself

It is fairly obvious that top performers believe that we are a product of our culture, upbringing, self-education, chronic thinking, and makeup. Even greats such as Dr. Carl Jung believed that we all have embedded talents and desires. As an example, President Obama wrote and spoke much of his ethnic makeup, ancestry, and childhood religious upbringing, and even President Trump talks sometimes about his family and his Scottish mother, Mary MacLeod Trump. He quotes her as saying, "Trust in God and be true to yourself," which are two very important things. Often, leaders will say that you *must* do something if it's important to you and to be bold and authentic, staying true to your core beliefs.

13.   Ready, Aim, Fire

We all have faced obstacles, enemies, competitors, and arguments. Top performers imply that we should pick our challenges carefully, picking our aim with intent. Choose your chief purpose, your chief aim in life, and then commit to it until you finish. There's a many "P's" that success gurus talk about in their books: purpose, poise, patience, perseverance – all of these concepts are important, because all of us have different goals in life, whether it's a small goal or a big goal. It's good to learn to commit to something and never look back and finish that goal as best you can. Moreover, the drive for the other P's can be both constructive and destructive; thus, we should all be careful of our quests for popularity, power, prestige, passion, and pesos. Even T. Boone Pickens, who I also met once many years ago, says that we should get ready, aim, and FIRE and not to sit around waiting to pull the trigger.

14.   Follow Your Heart and Passion to Authenticity

Ralph Waldo Emerson is famous for talking about the power of your ideas. Specifically, the greatest parts of your mind where you can put these ideas into action to help humanity. Further, Emerson really talked a lot about not following the crowd so much, not being a part of the herd but trying to be true to yourself. Whether you're an individualistic type of person with individualistic types of ideas, you can have a valuable contribution without just following the crowd. You can pick your own mission, chose your own destination, and be authentically successful doing what you love. When I was a young man, I sat next to Truet Cathy by accident on a commercial flight. Mr. Cathy told me about his chicken sandwiches, skillfully selling me on his great company. A few days after the flight, I received a letter from him with some gift cards. He was a true salesman and a real believer in his purpose. It is said that he did more for charity and orphans than any almost other American in history.

15.   Loyalty and Excellence is Always Recognized

Great leaders appreciate loyalty and emphasize being loyal as a: leader, follower, worker, staffer, or upper-level executive. An intelligent and loyal person will be recognized, but you've got to remember that some of us aren't built for certain types of companies or jobs. That's just the way it is. The famous management consultant Peter Drucker said, "If you work for a large organization for a few years you'll know whether or not you're built for it." Thus, keep your integrity, and people will judge you by your actions.

16.   The World is Constantly Changing

Adapt to the flux. Great leaders teach about opportunity, ideas, and preparation, and all of us should be ready for chaos and change, because there will always be ups and downs and chaos. If you look for opportunities, sometimes when there's chaos, there is opportunity. When there's an opportunity out there and you meet it with being prepared, that's when real genius and real luck occurs. However, remember that sometimes the road ends or changes, and we need to learn to re-brand ourselves, re-tool ourselves, keep reinventing ourselves and keep retraining ourselves. We've got to keep showing up and doing our best.

17.   How Will You Contribute Best?

Really, with all of that in mind, it's easier to succeed than it is to fail; because if you take care of yourself and do the right thing, good things will happen. In the twenty-first century economy, we all need to be focusing on how we can make our best contributions to the community and to humanity in general.

Your contribution could be from selling a tool, product, or service to help people have better lives or to saves lives, but sometimes we have to be realistic and just do our bread-and-butter work so we can take care of ourselves, be self-reliant, and take care of our loved ones. Many leaders emphatically say that we've got to keep our passions and hobbies. We can do the things we love to do on nights and weekends, outside of the scope of our general day-to-day work.

18. Focus on Producing while Keeping Healthy Hobbies.

Let go of the distractions. Just because you love music or a certain sport – it doesn't mean you can make money at it. There are just some people who are going to be better no matter what. But you can play golf, you can play music, you can travel, but we do need to focus on how we can best serve the world with our talents and our abilities at the same time.

I remember being in the gym one morning in New Orleans in the early 1990s. I was on a renewed health kick and working out hard. As I walked into the gym, I noticed it was just me and one giant man. We talked and worked out for forty-five minutes. Nobody else was there, and it was a bit strange. Later that morning, I discovered that I had worked out with Magic Johnson, but nobody was there because they were fearful of catching his HIV. In retrospect, it is amazing that they have found treatments to make diseases very manageable. Maintaining our health is vitally important, and once we find out we have a problem, it is important to do all we can to take care of ourselves. Today, Mr. Johnson is more successful than ever.

19.   Learn To Finish Well with Continuous Improvement

If you're new to success or if you're young, starting over, or just starting out, gurus like T Harv Eker talk about getting out there, just learning to do something, getting into your groove, and learning to finish something. Just commit to something and finish the job and do it well. Everyone knows that once you've done something for thirty days or sixty days, whether it's going to the gym, running a race or whatever it might be, when you finish the finish line, you've done something. If you've completed some task or built something, whether it's building a fence or digging a ditch and doing a great job – it doesn't matter. The top performers talk about the seed of success. Completion creates a new energy, a new flow and momentum that has to be looked at very keenly, very seriously.

Ponder on your ideas and act on the good ones. Peak performers say that once you finish something, then you have to move on to the next chapter in life, and you have to think about ideas and sit still, maybe gain some inspiration or talk to other people and try to be inspired from them. Be excited about life! Be eager – eager to learn, do, ask questions of others, and ask questions of yourself.

20.   What Would You Do?

What would you want to do next? What do you want to do with your free time? What would you do if you couldn't fail? Success gurus suggest asking ourselves these types of questions. Some billionaires have asked themselves, What lies behind you? What's in front of you? What are your goals/plans? What is calling for action within you? Do you have enough on the inside of knowledge and experience and willpower? Do you know how your dreams may evolve?

21.   Intuition and Serendipity

Even leaders such as the president say that you have to just allow life to guide you in different directions. Imagine you're stuck on a plane or train, or you're held up in some other way, and you're sitting next to somebody and you start talking. All of a sudden, you find out the greatest new idea, or you find out what's going on in the real world, maybe you hear some nugget of information that you need to know. So, sometimes, when you are guided or when things are changed, you have to be aware and look for the symbols, the signs, and the information, and be aware of your surroundings just in case something is trying to be presented to you. This is really about cultivating a little intuition, taking advantage of your higher perception, and maybe allowing a little adventure to create opportunity in your life.

22.   Importance of Self-Reliance and Maximizing Your Potential

On a more personal note, it appears that through the years of teaching and writing books, trying to help people maximize their potential, most self-help gurus tend to develop a strong belief in self-reliance from the standpoint that the more self-reliant people are, the better it is for the community, the churches, the hospitals, and the schools, and the better it is for the country as a whole. Thus, the more people who are able to take care of themselves, the more those in need will get help.

23.   Knowledge and Specific Literacy is Power

The guru philosophy also revolves around financial and regulatory literacy. Like many self-help writers, real leaders will talk about staying a student and continuing to be financially literate, success-literate, self-help literate, and literate with regards to health, body, mind, and soul. So, the gurus constantly talk about the more knowledge and experience you have, the better off you will be and the better decisions you'll be able to make.

24.   Change Provides Opportunity

Writers like Paul Zane Pilzer, T Harv Ekar, Tony Robbins, Larry Kudlow, and many other great people out there talk about how every time a huge collapse or a huge change occurs in society, there are lessons to be learned. Those moments teach us how to react, how to reinvest, how to re-tool, and how to regroup.

With the crash of 2000, we learned that technology wasn't invincible at that time. It took sixteen years for the stock market to come back from the Clinton Crash, which was the greatest stock market crash in history. The second biggest crash is the one that happened in 2008/2009, when Bush was transferring power to Obama.

In this chaos, we can learn a lot about real estate, risk, and investments. You've got to take a hard look at your investments and what's inside of them, knowing what the costs and fees are and what you're investing in. You can't just put your money in some fund and not know what it's about. The other thing is that sometimes economies change, and substitutes are created. As an example, we used to import a lot of oil and gas from other countries. Now, we're becoming more and more self-reliant. But when one industry sector changes, then we all need to learn how to adapt and reinvent and prevail. When energy is cheap, inflation slows and people in the transportation business make big money, and therefore disposable income for the people increases. Thus, while the oil and gas superpowers may make a little less, the dollars go to other places where opportunities for investment present themselves.

25.   Good Instincts – A Skill To Be Harnessed

One of the interesting words that some self-help masters use is the word *prescience*. It looks like "pre-science."

Really, this word is about having great instinct or taking advantage of a gut feeling or ideas that come from the inside. This is not necessarily about knowing the future, but rather just having good instincts about what decisions to make to increase the potentiality of success.

Gurus talk about how experience, knowledge, intuition, and inspiration are a great combination of mental powers. If you have learned experience and you've developed good knowledge from education where you also try and cultivate quiet time to become mentally be aware of your subconscious and conscious minds, all of these things will come together and allow you to be a very powerful thinker and decision maker.

With such a dynamic world of new technology and global interactions as we have in modern times, we must be aware when one door closes and another opens, being willing to learn from opportunities and mistakes. We must also be aware of detours, being able to take a preemptive strike for the huge changes that will inevitably come.

26.   Self-Respect and Self-Regard – The Inner Power

We must all cultivate self-respect and self-regard and be confident in ourselves. This is not to say we need to be egotistical; rather, we should have a quality ego consciousness with a sense of purpose. What is meant by saying "ego consciousness" is to have a healthy ego, one that can't be belittled or shamed by other people who are jealous of you or who don't want you to succeed. In the end, most powerful people advocate the art of knowing how to self-promote and humbly tell people about your successes, thereby allowing people to know your skills and your arts.

There was a famous book that I reviewed recently called *Brag* by Peggy Claus. I found this book to be helpful and insightful. We all must become our own "Master of the Brag," and Peggy Claus puts this formula in writing.

27.   Teamwork and Public Relations

With any successful person, you become a market leader. To be a market leader, you need a really sellable idea, and to sell it you must be aggressively truthful, take the high road, and believe in the product or service. You must learn to promote yourself as well as the other people with you. All of this is very, very important to the power of a unified and concerted PR stance.

28.   Great Ideas and Study – Keep Up With Your World

Victor Hugo says that there's one thing stronger than all the armies of the world, and that is an idea whose time has come. Top teachers encourage life-long learning and never looking at education as being a burden. They talk about how, with any new business or any new task or goal, there might be some new type of learning and preparation that needs to be done. We must cultivate the ability to think and use all of our power to maximize and develop that ability.

29.   Thankfulness

Winners and success gurus speak a great deal about gratitude and thanksgiving and having a thankful heart. They often speak of their parents and siblings with great reverence and love. President Trump even speaks of his deceased brother Fred as being a great teacher of what NOT to do. Before Fred died of alcohol-related issues, he had asked Donald not to get involved with alcohol. President

Trump heeded his brother's wishes. In the midst of successes, failures, and losses, it's extremely important to remain thankful for all the blessings that we've received and all the blessings that we may receive.

30.   Transcendental

With regard to being your best, many success gurus have great respect for some of the founding fathers and transcendentalist authors, such as Thoreau and Emerson. Really, at its core, I think that most super successful business people are trying to say that we should develop a higher consciousness and use that mental power in tandem with our actions. It's about being contemplative, mindful, and prepared while in action.

31.   What is Your Energy Level – How Will It Serve You?

Top gurus like Tim Fariss and Navy Seals are highly revered for their energy and work ethic. They say that many over-achievers decide to put in an extra three to four hours of work in each day. They figure that their performance will change as a result of this extra effort. If you do the math on it, if you put in another three or four hours of your day every day, then you've basically added another month to your year of productivity. It's an extremely important ideal if you can get by on four to five hours of sleep a day.

32.   Stay Aware and Keep Growing

Masters of high performance also profess at length about the concepts of perception, awareness, and mindfulness. With everything that you do, look at your strengths, weaknesses, opportunities, and threats, never becoming too complacent and always putting in your best effort. Always be mindful of when you need to adapt or change or take a detour to try to get over, under, or around obstacles. Be concise and on point in your work and presentations, and continue to learn and be curious.

True life coaches also talk about growth, and how we MUST keep growing in body, mind, and spirit. Always be mindful of your growth and your track record. It's true that sometimes growth is painful, and if you go to the gym and you work out really, really hard, you might be in pain the next day. But that's what growth is! We need to be vibrant and remain open to greatness and success. As we improve and see successes, we still must maintain industriousness to create even more opportunities. Sometimes, just by the fact that we're showing up early and leaving late, we're presented with more opportunities than we would have had before. One of the goals that leaders may be implying is to seek our uniqueness, meaning our own style, beat, and momentum, even leaving our comfort zones to do our absolute best.

33.   Life as an Art Form

Many leaders of great success see life as an art form. Really, at its core, every business is just like an artist's business. You've got to produce and paint something great that people want, that people are willing to pay for. So once that's done, and you have created something great, you've got to make sure that people see it! The more people have access to admire your work, the better odds that you'll get paid a fair value for that master creation. This applies to real estate, politics, jewelry, literary works, and most all businesses. I remember talking to Claus Obermeyer about necessities. He told me that his business started all because his wife had made him a down vest to keep him warm. An immigrant saw the need for certain clothing in the USA, and so the Sport Obermeyer company was born.

34. Wisdom

Wisdom is one of the highest virtues. Even in the Bible, King Solomon becomes the wealthiest man in the world by asking his God for wisdom—a combination of experience and knowledge. If you have wisdom, you will become wealthy. There have been many great books written on wisdom and strategy, such as Machiavelli's *The Prince* and Sun Tzu's *The Art of War*.

Another interesting facet about leaders is that they respect their ancestors' culture and traditions. Many leaders study their ancestors and understand the talents of their forefathers. People engage self-discovery, study their ancestry, and maybe even travel to the sacred villages or sites of their ancestors.

When we analyze our ancestors and where we're from, we open doors to learning about different cultures, mindsets, and types of things that people did in different parts of the world. It allows us to study history and be students of that history, absorbing information about culture, military history, immigration, and more.

35.   Don't Be Afraid or Ashamed of Winning

Many, many people are just scared or too timid to allow themselves to be victorious and enjoy it, or to simply be a good winner. Being a winner means doing a great job one day at a time, being the best you can be "in the now." Just one step at a time, one golf stroke at a time, one surf board ride at a time is all it takes while understanding your environment and doing your best.

36.   The Now

Another question that luminaries like Dyer, Tolle, or Chopra might ask a seeker is, "What's your mindset?" so that you can analyze your performance each day while paying attention to success. Look at your own ability to respond to the world. Again, many masters seem to emphasize the importance of the "now" and concentrating all of your efforts on the work at hand. Just do your best now, at this moment. Remember, the now creates the future and your actions and thinking in the NOW are what drive you toward your destiny.

37. Business Really is an Art Form and Negotiating is Like a Complex Dance With a Partner Who May Not Know How To Dance Like You Do

Doing your homework and being prepared are really nine-tenths of the builder's craft; so, life really is about cultivating your signature craft. If you look at any top author such as Napoleon Hill, Dale Carnegie, Zig Ziglar, or any of the other top peak performance authors, they will ask you, "What is your goal? What is your aim? What are you shooting for? What is your vision? What is your 'why', your essence? Why are you doing it?" People sometimes say, "I want to make X amount of money," but what are you going to do with the money once you get it?

It's good to know what you are going to do if you succeed, or how you going to be or live if you succeed. Clarify your intentions and thoughts, write them out, clarify your visualizations within your mind, and then learn to put it all together and remain well-educated. This will allow you to synthesize information to take action on a daily basis.

Really, the key here is continuous learning. When you have experience, you have knowledge, you have the ability to see different variables that are going on, and you are able to synthesize or combine the information to see a bigger picture.

38.   Obstacles

Philosophers and leaders say that sometimes you just can't label something as good or bad or give every obstacle a bad name. Often, we just have to identify a concern or challenge that we need to get around, rather than to fear it with some problematic character. That being said, we need to break down the concerns we have for every obstacle. Outline the objective issues or pieces and then try and determine a path to success that navigates around or through those obstacles. We can always compartmentalize each day with focus on the tasks at hand or compartmentalize the actual obstacle and work to get around it.

Then, we need to know what we are getting or doing before we are implementing something. We must to learn to diagnose issues so that we can arrive at a plan so that we know how to act before we actually start the action.

Careful planning means understanding the consequences of actions going out for days or even years. So, many philosophical minds, such as the Stoics, Transcendentalists, Native Americans, or the Prosperity Gospel followers really believe that fear feeds a counterproductive part of our mind, and that it is a part of your consciousness that doesn't need to be fed. So, we should replace the weakness attitude with one of power, confidence, and faith.

39. Developing a Big Picture

A mental big picture is the art of using applied visualization. This skill is about learning to focus the mind and to see the potential consequences and outcomes of any decision. If you take certain actions what will happen? Better yet, learn to truly see the actual final success in your mind's eye. With that being said, that final picture of success in your mind can actually help you develop actionable ideas toward the successful end result.

40.   Success is a Combination of Aptitude, Work, and Opportunity, and a Little Good Fortune.

If you always do more than what is expected, and you have acquired the skills that you need to engage in what you want to do, then you will develop a reputation and business art form that others will respect, and your creativity will be esteemed. We all need to mindful of how to be a deliberate, focused, intentional person who works smart and who works hard. Additionally, we should aspire to find our authentic expression in our work, our authentic style, and our passion. Be yourself, get the job done, be excellent, be prepared, seek opportunity, and providence will be presented to YOU.

41.   One Day at a Time

As a builder of great companies, most billionaires can give a great lecture on getting tasks done, completing goals, and having the right mindset. Every trained project manager knows that, for each goal, we must diagnose the problem and put together a plan and then work on each task at hand to implement that plan with focus, responsibility, and teamwork. The next step is to self-appraise the situation for continuous improvement. Having these skills is important, but being able to focus "one day at a time" and "one task at a time" are essential, because laser focus and daily achievement add up fast to great successes.

42. Communications

Develop good communications skills and an ability to sit down and clearly explain yourself to another person or to a group of people. This skill involves being able to take complex information and distill it down into common denominators that everyone can understand. Further, getting to the point and being concise, not beating around the bush, is a strong point advocated by any investor from Silicon Valley to Hong Kong. Thus, mastering the art of efficiency in communications will help you hit the points of your target. Some cultures, such as the Swiss, demand preparation before any meeting; thus, everyone wants to get the facts and have the due diligence completed to learn the most important information in the most effective and efficient way.

43.   Achieving Greatness

Many leaders discuss, with emphasis, the art of being excellent and achieving greatness. All great achievements are possible with a positive attitude, awareness, and clarity. Still, we must be dedicated to realistic solutions. All great achievements are based on perseverance and having a consciousness of success. We believe that most successful leaders understand that all people have their own unique style and their own unique flair. Even Google advocated that employees spend a portion of each week toward their passions and innovation. If you're going to be an employee within a large organizational chart, naturally you're going to have to do what is asked of you and perform and get results. But, I think the most successful companies encourage individuality.

You only need to watch great tennis players like Rafa Nadal, Roger Federer, or the Williams sisters to see that each one has their own style, their own flair. Each master has the type of clothes they feel best in, the type of racquets they use, shoes, equipment, mental preparedness, workouts, exercise, etc. They even each have their own rituals before, during, and after their games. Moreover, they play their best using their own game; they don't play other people's games.

14.   Self-Appraisal

With every winner, there is a process of self-inventory, and I think that leaders from Ben Franklin to Napoleon Hill and Dr. Stephen Covey all try to look at people and convey a message that each person should try and develop a track record of positive results to improve upon. It's almost like a resume or a curriculum vitae—you're trying to build assets, respectable achievements, a quality track record, and positive results. You should be able to itemize those things; write them down, list them, and be able to articulate them to others so you can maximize your highest talents and VALUE.

15.   Quiet Time, Mindfulness, and Contemplation

Some of the most powerful leaders advocate retreats to rest or bond with groups. Many of the most successful believe in quiet reflection and recharging the spirit. This can be done each day for a few minutes or as little as each year. Generally, all of us need to take time to unplug and have peaceful time to relax or meditate and sit still. It seems like most gurus are accentuating the fact that we can take even just a few minutes each day to relax and quiet our mind, which will build inspiration and tune us into the power of our minds and the universe. This is how many great thinkers, whether Edison or Einstein, have been able to sit down and decipher problems or come up with new ideas to solve big challenges or get around big obstacles.

The greats practice contemplation by sitting down and allowing their brain, both conscious and subconscious, to do some of the work for them. You, too, can harness this power.

46.   Momentum and Authenticity

If you read about Lincoln, Roosevelt, Emerson, and Thoreau, or any of the other great writers, you've learned that we have to be authentic, be ourselves, and listen to our heart. It's true that we should be authentic, but we also need to be effective. In essence, we must do all things well each day. And if you do three things well each day, then that adds up to momentum, and at the end of the year you've done over a thousand things great. Thus, this is a part of thinking big and thinking of the long-term while being patient.

47.　Persistence

We all know the story of the tortoise and the hare. The slow steady turtle beats the fast creature in a race by taking one methodical step at a time and focusing on the mission and destination. Thus, after finding what you need to start early, try, and finish early, work hard to maintain a sustainable, effective way of doing things in a reasonable way that does not involve waste. This IS a path to success.

Know what your creative assets are and use them to the best of your ability. Know what makes you valuable to yourself and others, and use those attributes to be the most determined person in your field.

48.　Your Legacy

Have you ever targeted or itemized what do you want to be known for? This is something that Ben Franklin talked about over two hundred years ago by focusing on excellence. It's something Dr. Stephen Covey of the "7 Habits" talked about just a few years ago in his bestsellers. Your legacy is: what do you want people to say about you when you're gone? What do you want to be known for? Do you want to be known for somebody who's sober, sharp, and upright, or you want to be known as somebody who's unfit and smokes and drinks too much? This is just an example.

49.　Inspiration

If we learn to use instinct with inspiration and logic, we can really approach great genius in word and deed.

Use your mind and your gut. Utilize your consciousness, your subconsciousness, and your gut instincts. While many great leaders refer to instincts in the same way that some of us might refer to intuition, it's sort of the same thing. Sometimes we just get that feeling and we know what we are supposed to do.

And if you can learn how to use all those thinking powers simultaneously, that can help you be a great person. Most success writers say that most of us are only using a small portion of our mind power. Really developing the use of your consciousness, subconsciousness, instincts, inspiration, and intuition can help you act accordingly right now, today!

50.　Art of the Sale

Every great leader knows about marketing, and I think it's because their whole lives have been devoted to preparing products and services to be sold to those who need solutions. In the end, you can have the greatest product or solution in the world, but if nobody sees it, you will never sell anything. If you can't explain the product, nobody will buy it. Thus, sales experts are needed. This is also why some masters need a right-hand person who can coordinate sales, marketing, and PR. Remember, the secret is getting to the common denominator of what people really want, particularly smart or affluent people, and relating this common denominator to the audience and to the customers. You need to be able to explain, "This is what's best for you" and why, and find out who your target is and target those people.

Honestly, life is an art form, and being able to convey your art to other people in the best way is one path to great success. Like they say, even a great artist is willing to reproduce a great piece that looks similar to the one before it if it has great appeal to the best people.

51. Chaos and Catastrophe

A great leader comprehends the need to maintain poise and calm when chaos comes. Be prepared for when that chaos comes. Think of it as a chess game – develop some ideas of moves you might make if something bad happens. This is called a "preemptive strike." Even great Olympians will sometimes prepare for the worst in case something happens during their competition. For example, if a piece of equipment malfunctions, how will you deal with that?

With any great entrepreneur, being prepared, staying calm, maintaining humility, not fighting against the forces that are out there, adapting as best you can, and then seizing opportunities are qualities they possess. You know that there are people out there who have made fortunes after the collapse of the economy, buying real estate, or after an S&L bailout they went out and bought a bunch of apartments and did great. This is the same idea: you seize these opportunities when they arise and don't fight against them.

Thus, the success gurus articulate that when we are prepared for opportunities to present themselves, this is equivalent to luck. Many great writers have talked about chaos as an equivalent to opportunity for many people. If you're prepared for chaos and opportunity, then that's when great things happen.

52.   Street Credibility

Successful leaders provide sage advice about building your street credibility, your reputation, and your integrity. There are several steps to getting street credibility, but a few of them are being a continuous learner and building your intelligence, learning to focus in an area and becoming a specialist, being responsible and having the ability to respond to situations, and being loyal either to yourself, to your company, or to the people you work for. Further, being authentic and being a results-oriented person where good is not good enough is another aspect of building street credibility.

53.   Getting Rich

Everyone wants to know how to get rich, and a billionaire's views are much in line with the views of many entrepreneurial Americans and bestselling authors. The richest people in the world teach that a lot of our ability to become prosperous is in the mind, cultivating the mental powers of being able to think and act with informed intelligence while keeping your mind persistent, and keeping the momentum.

If you have ever read the books by Emerson, Jung, or other great authors and visionaries, they know that we can all be the best at certain things. We can all perform better at things that are more in line with our passions and desires. Many top management consultants say we all have unique and innate talents, drives, and desires. Thus, if you maintain a positive mindset and can work hard, learn, do the right thing, and maintain your reputation of results and integrity, then you're probably going to do well in life.

But again, if you've read books by Napoleon Hill and other great writers, they talk about discovering what is your purpose, what you really want to do, and how you want to do it, and heading in that direction without looking back. That's really about your burning desires or your chief aim or purpose.

Then, once you've discovered what your chief aim in life is, your work will become a labor of love; it could be being the best writer, teacher, golf player, etc. It doesn't matter— when you find out what that is, then you devote your time and focus on that, work as efficiently and as effectively as you can, use action, and maintain your pace. Manage your time, focus on your work, and finish the job to the best of your ability. You will maximize your potential and excellence.

A lot of success has to do with the ability to work with other people and to cultivate relationships, to reach out, ask, knock on the door, and receive when someone offers you something. All of these things are pretty obvious, but top leaders talk a lot about keeping the right people, places, and things in your orbit around you so they can help you and you can help them in return.

54. Tithing, Charity, and Flow

One of the things about some billionaires that's not talked about is their unbelievable dedication to charity, giving back, and tithing, including people like Oprah Winfrey, Donald Trump, or the great Truett Cathy of Chick-fil-A who gave 10% his entire life, and people like the Carnegies, who gave great money to charity to build the US library system.

Many of the most charitable folks don't advertise or promote the fact that they continue to give to charity like hospitals, churches, temples, schools, and individuals who need medical care. They always seems to have a track record of tithing to people and communities that divinely inspire them. Most of the super rich earnestly believe that giving continuously to charity or to programs that divinely inspire you is the key ingredient to financial FLOW in their lives.

55. Labor of Love – Going the Extra 1%

The great human performance experts such as Dr. Napoleon Hill, constantly reiterate being specific with your intentions, knowing your purpose, and finding a labor of love. They speak of discovering your true aim, your passion, staying focused, and trying to outwork others while having fun doing it. Similarly, as great authors like Zig Ziglar talk about the difference between a great success and a failure can be a 1% or 2% extra effort.

So, if you always put in an extra little 1% or 2% a day, you're probably going to outsmart the rest of the people, particularly if you're doing a good job and effective and efficient type of performance. So, find out what your passion is. What's your blueprint look like? What do you want to do? Is it medicine, law, sports, technology? It doesn't matter what it ends up being, it's about discovering what makes you enthusiastic, what makes you feel ALIVE, and what energizes you.

56.   The Builder – All Creation Begins with an Idea

As you may remember, many leaders are mental builders at heart. For all of us out there, whether you're building websites or building schools, it's all a different type of artwork, different types of creation. So, when you build things you have to think about what's at stake there and how to make quality work. How do you create value? How do you create an increase for the buyer?

If you've read great self-help authors from over the last hundred years, they talk about the law of increase and conveying value to customers. I really think the greatest salesmen, such as Steve Jobs, have an earnest desire to provide amazing things for people. And if customers pay a lot more than what's expected, it's because they feel like their lives are increasing as a result of what the builder is providing. That's the real signature of a real leader—being able to build things that people really want or are willing to pay a little extra for.

57.   Empathy with Aggressive Energy

Great spiritual leaders and business leaders speak about being compassionate, empathetic, and using the powers that you have to be kindhearted towards others but staying hungry for excellence. They talk about staying aggressive and keeping that underdog mindset. Be confident, yeah, but always keep that underdog mindset and make sure you understand who and what you're competing against.

Even in this day and age, you may not just be competing against your neighbor down the street or some guy from another state; you might be competing with other people from 180 different countries. In the end, when you deal with other people or you deal with customers or buyers, you're trying to create win-win deals where mutual compromise sometimes is the best way to get closure on any deal.

58.   Trust but Verify – Keep the Keys to the City

This section is about hiring good people. I mean, hire the best people you can. Incentivize great employees or affiliates, do great things for them, make sure they want to work with you and be a part of the team. If you can, make sure they're team players by giving them clear rules of the game and a path to win. If they're not team-oriented players, make sure they've got valuable skills that they can share with the organization.

More importantly, you've got to have backstops and protection on everything related to your business: property, risk, and finances. You just can't trust people with the keys to the city. Make sure you're in control of your bank accounts and passwords, control your email and your agreements, accounts, rental space, registrations, domain names, and on down the line.

If somebody has too much access to your customer information, your technology, and your trade secrets, they can make a move and take advantage of your network and your money. So, take the time to do your research and hire great people so you can make sure you have control over the key assets and insure that nobody can hijack them just by walking out the door and starting a new company that looks just like yours.

59.   Goals, Objects and Ideals – Being Mindful of the Essence

Anybody can have a goal with a money number on it and say, "I want to be a millionaire" or "I want to make $100,000 this month", or whatever it is. Anybody can make up a financial goal with a number, and that's a good idea to have in life's game, which includes an exact number or a specific result, but on a metaphysical level, it's much more important to know the essence behind the number.

There's an old story that somebody prayed for $10,000 and soon thereafter they were hurt on the job in an accident, and the injured person got a $10,000 severance check. The moral of that story is to be careful what you pray for.

Pray or be mindful for something specific, but understand what you're going to do to receive this reward. For example, I want to help 10,000 people get a better education and learn how to be better people and reach their human potential. By helping these 10,000 people, I'm going to make a million dollars doing it. That's generally what is meant by the essence behind what you want. You can imagine yourself completing a task or finishing a race, or whatever it is, and that's perfect, but you have to understand what you are going to do when you finish the job, how you are going to finish the job successfully, and who am I going to help along the way or afterward in relation to this particular goal or task or objective.

60. Life-Changing Event

Another excellent point made by people who follow peak performance teachings is the fact that any one event or any one victory in life can change your life forever and make you a PLAYER. The teaching is: "You need to become that event" or be "at one with" that turning point in your life, and "target" a passion, excellence, or a dream that is going to put you in the big league.

61.   Brutal Honesty and Tough Love is Required Sometimes

This section really is about the reality of the world. The fact of the matter is that if you become successful, there are going to be people that admire you, and there are going to people that hate you no matter what. It doesn't matter where you go in life, whether you are a child or adult, when you walk into an establishment, there are going to be some people that just don't like the way you look. But don't focus on that! There are going to be some people that love the way you look. It doesn't really matter. That's not the point we're trying to make. The point is that, in the end, there's always going to be somebody who is jealous of you or wants what you have: your car, your clothing, your loved ones, your job, etc. It doesn't really matter.

Once you start moving up the food chain, there are people at the bottom of the food chain who are going to look at you like you are a target, and there are going to be mean and smart people who are going to try and separate you from your success, money, and happiness. Protect your body, your mind, and your soul.

Learn how to protect your mindset (in some countries, they might say to protect your Energy). This is because all great people, all successful people have a powerful mind and a powerful brain, but you need to protect it from these people who want to suck your energy, taking from you instead of giving you something of value in return.

So, really, the high level operating people, people operating at a higher level mentally, know how to protect their mind and their heart from problem people and at least try to avoid toxic situations. Many self-help gurus out there will say that half of life's luck is avoiding: bad people, places, things, and toxic situations. It's just a fact that avoiding belligerent imbeciles and other traps is half of life's luck.

62.   Make Your Reputation as a Fighter Known

Another fascinating point that supercharged people make is that you have to know how to be an open-minded person who listens and is helpful in business, but you can't be a pushover, either. The point of the lesson here is that you can't be other people's doormat. If you're in a competitive business where there are a lot of other businesses competing for the same thing, you really have to know how to defend yourself and not take crap from other people. If somebody does something wrong to you and you have a cause of action, you need to get a lawyer or report it to the authorities. Take care of it!

Show other people that you're not going to be the type of person to accept some abusive situation. If somebody tries to sue you, for instance. Let's say you're in the wrong and they're in the wrong, but they're in the wrong <u>much more</u> than you, you countersue and hit them with everything you've got. You hit them with as many charges and as many counts, as many claims as you can. You try and hit them for compensatory damages, punitive damages, and treble damages. You get that issue filed in court, which becomes public and makes your opponent look very bad, particularly if you have a good case. Even if the offender is in Australia or China, you find a way to assert jurisdiction over the offenders and make them pay and drag them into court in the USA.

That's just the legal world that we're in. Never let other people get one over on you, particularly if you have the edge and leverage. Now, say somebody comes at you and they're suing you, and they clearly have all the leverage, then figure out how to get out of the case as quickly as you can and settle it with a win-win deal, particularly if it's going to be a waste of your time and energy. There are some cases that are just crap, though, and you'll know the difference. But don't let some "run-of-the-mill lawyer" convince you that you have a good case unless you really do.

53.   Make People Happy to Work for You

There are many ways to inspire people. No matter what business you're in, whether you're a doctor, lawyer, selling clothes, selling books, or whatever, it doesn't matter. There will be other people helping if you want to be GREAT, and you'll want to try and help other people to help you sell and promote a business, product, or service that you have. The more people you have helping you, the more eyes that might see your product or service. The possibility for success in sales and for making an honest living or helping people increases, and you receive some type of compensation for it.

So, the logic behind all of this is that you've got to figure out how to incentivize people. If there's a way to split the rewards, give everybody a commission on something that they're selling for you – don't hesitate, DO IT. As they say in many countries in Asia and other places, if there's a way to cut somebody a little margin, DO IT. If people are working hard, you will want them to be emotionally involved in helping you. Basically, margin means commission, or a little percentage, and if there's a way to cut them in, do it. That's how Amazon, Google, and all these other internet companies have become so big. Basically, for many years during the internet growth, internet companies had a lot of people doing what's called affiliate sales, having somebody promote their products and services through links and pages and everything else with free advertising, and they gave those resellers a little piece of the pie. After a couple of years, internet companies let a lot of these people go and got rid of certain reselling mechanisms, which led to commission-based sales. Thus, much of the marketing for the internet greats was done by little people on the ground. I'm just saying that free and incentivized marketing is big. It is the same with brokers or insurance companies who will hire agents to boost PR to family and friends. If they are successful, you keep them; if not, let them go.

If anybody does an excellent job, and if anybody's really selling, whether it's for Amazon or Google or anybody else, they are making the company money and they're going to buy you out. They're going to make sure you get paid, particularly if you're doing a great job. So, it's a two-sided street. Do a good job, and that's how you can become rich. In any sales position, it's an untold truth that there is an unlimited number of possibilities.

64. Get It in Writing – Think Ahead – Exit and Risk Strategy

We are now talking about protecting yourself with legal documentation. It doesn't matter if it's just family or a spouse, as a lot of people talk about prenuptial agreements and protecting yourself in marriage and all that. That's fine. If your husband or wife or whatever wants to sign, or a fiancée wants to sign one of those agreements, then that's fine. A lot of people bring assets into the marriage whether they inherit it or not. Those things belong to you, but you might want to find ways to protect separate assets as well through some type of agreement or keep it separate under the local and state laws that allow separate property to be kept.

But, there are lots of other types of LEGAL documentation that are just as important. If you're in a partnership with someone in business, whether it's in services, restaurant, small business, law, medicine, insurance, or other area, you're going to want to have a prenuptial "business" agreement with your partners.

It's not called a prenuptial agreement, of course, but it might be called a buyout agreement, operating agreement or something of that sort. If your partner dies, for example, you get a chance to buy out their stock, or you may have some mechanism in place where you can buy out the shares or have the right of first refusal. Whether it's in an LLC document or a corporate document, these types of terms can be added.

Particularly with family, if you've ever studied wealth

management or listened to a financial management lecture, everybody needs to have a will, maybe even a living will or a healthcare directive, etc. Thus, there are all these things to protect you or your loved ones in case you're incapable of managing your affairs and you need someone else to do it for you, or if you become sick. There are many other things that might be really smart moves for you, such as making sure you can buy health insurance. If you're healthy, buy life insurance. If you're healthy, also try and get some disability insurance if you can afford it, because you never know what's going to happen. There's a certain amount of risk out there no matter what. Your health is the most important thing.

65. Get Quality and Buy First Class if You Can

This law is just about buying QUALITY. Anybody who's reading or listening right now remembers going to the store during your life, and you looked at an expensive pair of shoes, and then you looked at another pair of shoes that was a little less, and you bought the pair of shoes that was a little less. Then, in the end, the pair of shoes that was a little less didn't look quite as good, didn't last quite as long, and certainly weren't comfortable enough on your feet. Sometimes you better just go ahead and buy a pair of shoes that cost three or four hundred dollars, or even nine hundred! I don't know what a great ladies shoe costs, but great handmade shoes start out probably three to four hundred in cash right now, in 2017.

I remember back when I was a young law student working in a building in downtown, there was an old attorney there who had some custom-made shoes from London. One pair was twenty-two years old, and another pair was twenty-five years old, and they still looked brand new. He had them shined and conditioned at least once a month and took them off the moment he got home. He had them custom fit where he had some company make a mold of his foot in London, and he had the shoes mailed to him. About every ten years he had a new pair. It was unbelievable! The same holds true with a nice belt, jacket, car, suit, and on and on it goes.

One story that President Trump tells is about buying some sports team that is valuable. He says, if you buy, go for the big league and get a hold of a real team that's first rate, you know, whether it's an NFL or an NBA team, and it's always going to have value because market leaders always maintain their value. And, the same holds true with the property. If you're in a great part of town, whether you're in the smallest house or the largest house, those well-situated properties usually maintain their value.

56.   Your Image and Brand

Be a high-level person in the way you speak, the way you handle yourself, the way you hold yourself up, and the type of people you surround yourself with. All of these attributes are incredibly important. Further, not everybody has the ability to look perfect, but, certainly, taking care of yourself, your body, your hair, your teeth, your skin and everything else is very, very important.

It just goes back to the old story of the Beatles. Back when they were starting out, you know, the manager went out and got them some nice outfits and made them look good and cleaned them up, and that's just the way it is. The flipside of that is whether any rock and roll star will tell you back when he was young, he wanted to hire an agent who looked good, drove a nice car, and had a nice suit.

It's just the same old story, and most people don't want their lawyer, priest, or doctor to look weird or drive an old broken-down car. They want their agents and employees and bosses to look good, fit the part, and look like a success. It's just the way of the world. So, the moral of the story is to think of yourself as important. Believe you're important and organize yourself like you're important.

67. What's My Value – What Have You Done For Yourself Lately?

The hardest thing to do is to take a hard look at yourself and, each year or every six months, you have to take a hard look at yourself and take an inventory and find out what makes you worth a lot to other people. What are your top hobbies and talents? How are you willing to use these things to better your community and humanity and make your life better for you and your loved ones?

Then, you have to be bold and being proactive, getting out of your comfort zone, taking steps to make your life better and to improve yourself. Moreover, be objective, listen to other people, and maybe ask for other people's opinions about how to go forward. Keep your eyes open and aware to the changes in society and humanity or the different needs of people from around the world. All these might provide different opportunities for you to provide your human capital and your value to other people.

In the end, you have to try and learn who you are. Know thyself, but also know who your people are that are helping you and what their capacities are and know how to talk to them and ask them to be their best. But also, you need to know how to synthesize or synergize information from your actual assets for the best results; really taking into consideration all the different variables around you, whether it's in a negotiation or the completion of a project on a day-to-day basis, or to actually be meeting your goals at the end of the year, the end of five years, or the end of ten years.

68.   The Art of Any Deal – Thoughts on the Trump Bestseller

1. Know who is involved – The parties

2. Know the purpose of the deal

3. Know the terms

4. Know who does what – Who is responsible for implementing the deal

5. How long is the deal?

6. What is the bargain? Who pays what?

7. Understand the how and when to assent to the deal and make it a meeting of the minds where the agreement is binding.

8. Is the deal insured or protected?

9. Know how to get out of the deal.

10. Know how the deal is protected from harm, injury, or insured, etc. What is your exit strategy of selling or moving on?

11. Aim high in asking for what you want and be willing to settle the deal on mutually beneficial terms.

12. Be Flexible: Most leaders say to never get too attached to one deal or one investment.

13. Know your market

14. Find leverage and use it.

15.   Keep the deal sustainable with costs.

16.   Fight for what you want.

17.   The deal is to create quality services or products.
Thus, you must be able to deliver value.

69.   Working Hard – Having Great Energy and Winning

Persistence pays off. It takes one step at a time, one day at a time. Patience. If we keep chipping away at our goal, we come closer to its reality each day. There may be people faster than you, a bit smarter than you, but nobody can outwork you if you put your mind into focus and into the zone. Keep your mind, heart, and attention right, and the rest will follow. As Zig Zigler, the great sales guru, has implied, there is only a 1%-2% difference in the performance between the greatest in the world and others who never achieve anything.

70.   Luck and Haminja

Another interesting thing about a WINNING mindset is that some people are just a little bit luckier than others, believe in themselves just a little bit more, and believe in their abilities a tad more than others. If you've ever studied

Eurasian mythology, there are some tribes in the North, like in the old Norse mythology, where the ancient peoples believed that some children are born with a certain amount of luck from their forefathers. It's almost part of their DNA, and maybe there's some truth to that. *In Norse mythology, **hamingja** (Old Norse "luck") refers to two concepts: the personification of the good fortune or luck of an individual or family, and that it is an aspect of the soul or essence of a person.* It's a subset of a person's character and soul under the old mythological teachings. So, some people are born a little luckier or they have great charisma or MOJO, but the moral of the story is that the harder you work, the better you control your emotions, the more you know, and the harder you prepare, and then the luckier you probably become. That's just the way it is.

71.   Ideas and Belief

TAKE CONTROL OF YOUR MIND! All creation and goals begin with an idea. Our belief system about ideas and goals must be based on the probability of reasonably good results.

72.   Definitiveness of Purpose

Focus your heart and actions upon a definite, well-developed purpose as a life dedication. Overall, a definiteness of purpose of your plan along with a burning desire is generally what is needed to accomplish great things. When you mix this recipe with constructive belief or faith, you become driven to do what is necessary to succeed and NOT to give up. You believe that "You Can."

"Those who are not prepared for the apprehension of a great purpose, should fix the thoughts upon the faultless performance of their duty, no matter how insignificant their task may appear. Only in this way can the thoughts be gathered and focused, and resolution and energy be developed. Once this is done, there is nothing which may not be accomplished." James Allen

73.   Acceptance

We must believe that prosperity and well-being are our birthright. Believe that the possibility of abundance and riches is a reasonable option for your life's purpose and commitments. When your dominant thoughts revolve around your purpose, your overriding mental energy and chief aim will be a catalyst to the manifestation of what you desire. When firm belief, earnestness, and constructive emotion are behind a burning desire, the purpose is energized. We must understand the rationale behind our desires. Write out a list of who, what, when, where, and why we must achieve our goals and determine how it will help all who are involved.

74.   Self-Regard, Worthiness, and Confidence

With opportunity comes responsibility toward your mental, physical, and spiritual health. Do what works to take care of yourself with diet, exercise, learning, sleep, and fellowship. Prune habits that stand in the way of your happiness and health. This practice will instill a power of worthiness. Ask for help or a life coach if need be.

75.   Feed Yourself and Gain Mental Attunement

Nourish yourself with food, news, and information that can make you highly skilled, happy, successful, and healthy. Develop great routines and habits. Become excellent, simplify your life, empty the clutter, and refine your focus.

But before implementing each plan or taking any big step, evaluate your mental effectiveness. Getting clear and going through a mental catharsis will free our thinking abilities. This means looking at your track record, atone, prune, purge, and clear away the mental debris. Begin to master "what works best for you" and start to utilize the practices that make you efficient and healthy.

76.   Invest in Yourself and Prepare for the Future

Make a habit of investing in your own excellence. Spend time and money when it is an investment in yourself, your future, your business, your retirement, your education and travel, your loved ones, or risk management tactics.

77.   Right Livelihood and Labor of Love

Occupational analysis can turn work into play. Research ideas! What are your passions, how do your ideas serve you? What work would make you feel alive? Then, create plans, look at what it would take to be successful, then act on them, implement your strategies, and review and improve them each year.

78.   Action and Boldness

Having a clear mind that works creatively allows for big opportunities where commitments may be selected. Commitment creates a nucleus of new momentum and begins a chain reaction of creation. Each day will become an opportunity to move closer to achievement by doing each act or task in an efficient and effective manner. Do it right the first time and you will not need to do it again.

79.   Imagination and Visualization

Using the mind to picture and emotionalize your success is one of the golden keys to prosperity. This process allows you to see your future or pre-dream your destiny. You can effectively build what you want in your mind, saving years of time as a shortcut toward your ultimate successes. See yourself in optimal circumstances in your mind's eye and FEEL it. If you can visualize the most favorable result, then see the next step. Example: see yourself a few pounds leaner toward your optimal weight.

80.   Character Development

"YOUR Thinking" or what you think about habitually IS who you are and what you are made of. The totality of your thoughts and actions is your character. Radiate excellence, cheer, and zeal. Build yourself from the inside out, do each act with effectiveness, and others will see your great character and dedication to excellence. Make wealth and excellence a priority by aligning your thoughts with success, health, and prosperity.

81.   Enthusiasm

Enthusiasm will enable you to "saturate" all you meet with confident energy and compel others to be interested in both you and your ideas. Zeal is a key foundation of a pleasing personality, and you must have such a personality to influence others to cooperate with you. When belief, earnestness, and constructive emotion are behind a purpose, that purpose is energized and increases the probabilities of success and even luck. Be teachable, learn to receive from others, offer praise, and appreciate life. Learn to allow your spiritual and charismatic energy to support your ideas and goals.

82.   SELF-CONTROL

Discipline and self-control are engines that can steer you into great opportunities and away from problems. Determine who you want to associate with, have relationships with, and do business with. Keep lists and do three constructive things per day toward the fulfillment of your dreams to the best of your ability.

83.   The Law of Increase

When you provide service or products to others, you should convey the energy of increase to all. In this way, people know that when you are providing help, their lives and abilities are expanding. You are providing solutions to problems and easing the suffering of others by your service. Further, we must know and speak of ways in which our ideas and success will help customers and all others.

84.   A Constructive Attitude

Cultivate a pleasing and confident personality. Develop affirmations that assist in lifting your vibration to higher levels where you are perceived as somebody that others would want to help and cooperate with. As an example, "I am energetic, creative, whole, healthy and wealthy. I am rich with life and love." Become a beacon of abundance and excellence. Learn to think and speak in prosperous ways that convey confidence, opportunity, and cheer. Mold the habits and tendencies of your thought toward an attitude of well-being and optimism.

35.   Organized Thought

Having the power to direct your thinking will ultimately create your reality. Knowing the facts affects your ideas and actions. Do your best to have the most factual inputs and your outputs will be more accurate. What is thought about habitually becomes who you are and affects what you do, how you act, what you receive, and what you achieve. Think, feel, and act as if you are already in possession of what you want to obtain. Cultivate emotions and your character around YOUR mental pictures of victory and happiness.

36.   Contemplation and Quantum Leaps

Meditate and pray by writing out affirmative meditations, such as, "Each day I am improving." Write out ten statements that are affirming and positive and contemplate them each day. Ask for inspiration from your subconscious or from your divine connection. Seek to expand your life. Go past your comfort zones. List goals beyond your expectations and have specific deadlines. You can always change the dates.

87.   Monitoring and Inventory

Every outcome contains a lesson that is the seed of future success. Even if you fail, you learn invaluable lessons that may guide you to greater and greater heights. Study your days, reflect on your activities. Decide how to continually improve yourself. Do your homework and do all you can to learn and know your niche. Look at where you are, who you are, and where you are going, then you can periodically reset your course and navigate to optimize the journey. Devote twenty percent of your waking hours each week to your passion and creativity. If you become great at doing anything fun or creative, odds are you can also earn a living doing it.

88.   Harmlessness

Treat YOURSELF in a way that you would treat others. Treat yourself with dignity and high regard. Help others make the best of themselves. Teach others these steps and you will be able to help them live to their highest order. As they say, we must give it away to keep it. Learn to focus your days on constructive activities, and avoid senseless arguments with those who do not care about your success.

89.   The Third Force – Networking and Support Groups

This concept is timeless in that if two or more people are gathered, a third force of energy and creativity presents itself. Model yourself after successful people. Do what the winners do. Ask successful people for advice or insights. Join a local business or discussion group. Just keep in mind that you must carefully select those whom you ask to be part of your network. Make sure they have specialized knowledge, a good track record, and are supportive and encouraging.

90. Develop your Intuition and Sixth Sense

Learn and practice awareness, keep a journal, write out creative thoughts, develop and allow a universal flow of ideas into your mind. Continue to work these steps in all of your affairs while maintaining your purpose and dedication while helping others who want prosperity and peace of mind.

91. LESSONS

There are lessons in every mistake. If you read Dr. Napoleon Hill or Oprah Winfrey's work, you will understand that there is sometimes the seed of success in every failure. The great news with any failure or mistake is that you NEVER need to repeat it. You can move on to new heights.

92. The Magic of Words

Write your goals down. There is magic in those words. If you read the great ideas or top management consultants like Bryan Tracy, you'll see that there are scientific advantages in writing out your objectives. Include notes on places you want to see, things you want to do, skills you want to learn. If you do two or three things a day, then by the end of the year, you'll have a thousand things done. It is amazing how the mind works to allow the subconscious mind to assist us even while we are sleeping or resting. When you put an idea in your mind the deeper consciousness actually begins to work on the ideas, seeking solutions around the clock.

93.   Purpose and What you DON'T WANT

Great writers of history have often talked about cultivating a chief purpose or determining your labor of love. Generally, narrowing our focus and directing our energies can make us very powerful and boost our momentum. There is a flip side to this also. We all need to know what we want to do and to go after our desires and ideas with all of our efforts. However, you also need to know what you don't want in life and the types of activities that we need to get rid of. There are various types of actions or omissions to avoid to be successful. Some success gurus such as Stuart Wilde have claimed that "half of life's success" is avoiding toxic people. Moreover, the great Tony Robins has also taught that you need to know what you DON'T want, and then get a target of what you DO WANT, and go after it with extreme fervor and enthusiasm.

94. Start Early and Be On Time

Whether you're talking about Abraham Lincoln or Dr. Oz or the "tortoise and the hare," it's always best just to get started and get moving, and sooner or later you'll cross that finish line with great success. Even Abe Lincoln said if you gave him a few hours to chop down a tree, he would spend most of his time sharpening the axe. By doing this, you could take the tree out quicker, faster, and better without stress or haste.

95. Authenticity

To stay true to yourself, be authentic and remain teachable. One of the definitions of humility is to remain teachable, and if you have your ears and your eyes open, no matter how smart you are, no matter how many degrees you have behind your name, if you're smart and you're aware, you will learn things, and you might gather information that is priceless. Even Clint Eastwood in one of his famous Westerns said, "A man's life in these parts often depends on a mere scrap of information." Whether you read Socrates, Buddha, or Shakespeare, "Know thyself."

96.   Health

Put your mental, spiritual, and physical health first. Whether you're taking a class from somebody like the great Suze Orman, or if you're learning a lesson from another great teacher, you're putting your mental, spiritual, and physical health first, which essentially means you are investing in yourself. Taking care of yourself, developing self-love, developing self-regard, and more are invaluable steps. If you treat yourself well, you'll invariably be able to treat other people well also.

97.   The ZONE

Every year there are many self-help books released with a general theme and focus. One of the biggest themes in the last few years has been, "How to get out of your comfort zone." Encouraging people to go and do something different, learning to be something new, taking a new path, this is solid advice. Develop healthy routines and doing things well and right, not deviating from what works for you. However, there's also something to be said for taking calculated risks and getting out of your comfort zone. People like the great T. Harv Eker, who's an excellent author and an excellent speaker, has talked in length about this. Pick up the phone and call somebody who you want to meet or speak with, or call somebody and ask them for help as a mentor, saying, look, I know you've done this type of business before, you're great at it, can you help me, can you teach me what I need to know maybe to be good in this business too or a similar business? Therefore, reach out, try something new, and engage new activities that make you feel alive. This overall theme in many books is a very powerful message.

98.   Manage Your Mind

"Mind your business and manage your mind." If you read great books or listen to great speeches by sales gurus such as Zig Ziglar, you'll understand that we all need to "prime our pumps" to get our mind moving and focus on building our mind power every day. A lot of the great self-help authors talk about buying self-help tapes or reading books, having "learning CDs" in your car, or downloading audio books. In today's world, managing your mind has a much greater meaning in that we need to keep our mind clear and running smoothly, like getting oil change on a vehicle, or having a computer run a virus check, or deleting junk out of the cache or the temporary files of a computer so it can operate more quickly and respond and be more responsive. That's what we're talking about managing your mind. It's one thing to mind your own business, that means to focus on what you need to do for yourself and not what other people need to do. It's another thing to talk about the effective and efficient management of your own mind.

99.   PEACE OF MIND

The next principle is to become a conscious observer of your mind and of your ego. Famous writers on the subject of consciousness, such as Eckhart Tolle or Thich Nhat Hanh, talk a lot about learning to meditate or to quiet the mind where you become able to observe your thoughts and sharpen mental activity. But the next level beyond these teachings is learning to discern the difference between your spiritual consciousness and your ego consciousness. This is the ability to know what is good, constructive, and beneficial for YOU, and a harmonious action as compared to thoughts that are just destructive and selfish and that aren't going to get you anywhere, that wastes your time, or that wastes your mental energy. Mental energy is precious, and if you get bogged with just one resentment or one angry thought, you can spend half of your day or your whole day (some people are capable of spending weeks or years) being angry and upset, which basically wastes your time and your life, when you could have been a more productive member of society or spent more time with your children or family.

100. Healthy Routines

The next key to success is healthy routines and why you should have them. It doesn't matter who you are or what age you are, whether you're fourteen or ninety-two, it doesn't really matter. We need to eat right; sleep right; have healthy fellowship with other human beings, so we can continue to cultivate friendships and relationships and be able to express ourselves with others; and get the type of exercise that we need. Now, exercise can be broken down to several areas. There's physical exercise, mental exercise, and then the spiritual gymnasium. There's a nice blend between all of these things. If you pick up a book on anxiety or depression or even if it's ADHD or bipolar or any type of debilitating situation that an individual may have, you pick up a book on any of these things, whether it's addiction, it doesn't matter, there's going to be a couple of sections in the book about letting go of destructive habits and picking up constructive and beneficial habits in their place. Those aren't addictions, but rather constructive and beneficial activities. Activities that make you feel alive, that give you joy to benefit your life and those you love are the keys to this step. There is a retired admiral that made millions of dollars with speeches and a book telling about getting up and making your bed in the morning. I believe the message is that we can learn to: "Do one thing right when you wake up and the rest of the day will continue to follow that expression of good will." Therefore, healthy routines of fellowship/social interaction, REM-quality sleep, exercise, and diet/nutrition are all very important. The acronym for fellowship, REM, exercise and diet, would be FRED. The scientific value to FRED is that they may all stimulate proper well-being, production of serotonin and dopamine, and also create a healthier body on a physical level.

5 Bonus Laws

Looking for even more inspiration and understanding? These five bonus laws delve further into improving your mind to be the best you can be.

101.   Responsibility

The next step is really about how to practice effective and rapid response and learning to do things well. I've known a few top surgeons in my life, and some can do an operation in thirty minutes and others it might take them three or four hours. Both surgeons are safe and not being negligent, not going too fast. To be honest, an "on-schedule and quick" surgery reduces the risk of infection and complications. But, different people are more comfortable doing things really well at different speeds. I think it takes practice, practice, practice to achieve new levels of skill. Recently, I heard a speech by Mike Singletary, the famous linebacker, and he said he practiced eye-mind awareness skills and rapid response using techniques that I had read that were used by "secret spiritual factions" hundreds of years ago. Singletary said he would stand up and take his two fingers and hold them out on each side and try to spread his awareness and depth perception by being able to see things in the corners of his vision to try to understand movements better. The great linebacker used these exercises to be able to see or READ the other team's offensive line much better than any other linebacker in our lifetime most probably.

This is about practicing rapid response, which is different than reaction. It's more of a conscious responsiveness. If you watched Tom Cruise and his famous movie, *Last Samurai*, his character was subject to the same interplay when they were telling Cruise to use "no mind," to keep practicing and developing his skills. By the end of the season, he was able to respond lightning fast with his sword with the utmost skill. I seem to remember the great time management consultant Tim Ferris talking a good bit about being able to do things really well. He uses an example of trying to respond to as many emails as effectively as you can within a certain amount of time and getting that part of your day behind you. As a Lawyer, I say be careful with emails and hasty responses, but for non-legal communications, it sounds like a great exercise.

102.   You Are What You SEEK

The next step is to regulate what you take in, both physically and mentally on a conscious level. If you read books by the great Dr. Deepak Chopra or many other great spiritual and self-help writers, you'll see that they talk about the types of negative information that you choose to take in and whether that is healthy for you. The types of people, places, and things that you encounter or allow yourself to encounter is also important. Are those interactions healthy for you? The next level beyond that is, "you are what you eat." In this day and age, in the new science of the twenty-first century, everybody really needs to find out what types of foods, diets, liquids, and quality of water they should be consuming. We are all slightly different in our needs, so if you're not feeling well, or maybe just feeling "off," go see a doctor or a nutritionist to discover what you need to be consuming. Mental health is one issue, but physical and dietary issues can affect the mind, and we must make sure that your body is at its optimum level.

Today, the talk out of Silicon Valley and the pro sports world is about brain hacking and peak performance. Young performers, like Tom Brady, are taking: various vitamins, minerals, and nutrition plans and eating certain things, like certain proteins and herbs, etc. to stay in peak shape. Some of the vitamins they take are even synthetic forms of vitamins, which may maximize their mental and physical condition. This is NOT steroids. We're not even talking about steroids, and we're NOT talking about SPEED, either. Whether it's Ritalin, Adderall, or steroids, this topic is NOT about the use of doctor-prescribed drugs.

In sum, there's a whole new Generation X out there that are monitoring and maximizing their mental, physical, and spiritual health through the use of testing, computers, diet, herbs, proteins, minerals, and vitamins, along with exercise, hired coaches, and everything else. It could be called a "buck shot approach" that people are using when they are trying to turbo-charge themselves physically, mentally, and emotionally. Be discerning about what you eat and you consume so you can maximize yourself each day, whether it be during the day or at night while you sleep. There are even things to do to improve your sleep, as well. Sleep is important because a good quality REM sleep is what allows your mind to function at its best the following day. Some people have specific foods, meditations, exercise, or supplements they do or take before they sleep to make sure they have a great sleep pattern.

103.   Be You and Be Alive

The next step is really to find out what makes you feel alive. Make a list of things that you enjoy doing, that you don't enjoy doing, or things you MAY enjoy doing. Go try them out if you can, or find somebody who is good at a particular activity you want to try out and talk to them. Say, "Hey, I know that you ski the mountain every year, would you take me with you and teach me?" There are lots of great hobbies to try in life. It's not just getting out of your comfort zone. This is really about learning new skills and being alive. Unless you experience or try certain things, sometimes it's difficult to know what really makes you feel good. Sometimes people fall into a certain type of job, or occupation, or labor of love when they didn't even know they enjoyed it, they just happened to experience it or go try it out. A lot of authors have talked about this. Sometimes you have to just go work at the donut shop to find out whether or not you enjoy dealing with pastries and customers every day. What makes you feel alive? What makes you feel wonderful? What gives you energy? What animates you in life? If you read great authors like Martha Beck, T. Harv Ekar, or any of the others, they talk a lot about this. Even Dr. Chopra talks about the word "Dharma" and your purpose in life and what animates you. In sum, this is about getting into your groove and finding where you can best operate, maximize your potential, and serve humanity.

104.   Your Environment

The next step is, who do you associate with? The famous Kim Blanchard and other authors talk about how attitudes rub off on us. They've analyzed various types people, in the United States and other places, and their income, happiness, and the success rate of the average person is about equal to or similar to the people that they associate with, generally speaking. So, if you can, associate with people who are smarter than you, faster than you, better than you, that maybe you can learn something from. Maybe it will rub off. Maybe it will allow you to strive to beat those goals and to do better and better and better. So, this is just another example. Surround yourself with people who can help you grow. Remember, there is something called vibration. If you put two tuning forks next to each other and ring one of the forks, the other fork will begin to vibrate at the same level. It's the same with us and who we associate with.

105.   What is Your Energy Type?

The last principle is to know your matrix. Really, this idea is about understanding and knowing yourself. Whether you go back to Shakespeare, Buddha, Jesus Christ, or any great philosopher, teachers, or masters of time and history, they're going to say to know yourself, particularly if you want peace of mind. Know who you are. Know your authentic self and connect with that authentic self. Emerson, Thoreau, and the like say don't be a "cow in the herd" just following the others. You can be unique, beat to your own drum, and be the best you can be. Maybe you can do something unique, different, and wonderful. Be who you're supposed to be. Remember, the unneeded cornerstone is always necessary in the end of the day to make the architecture complete and strong.

May the winds of prosperity blow the sails of success for you, as you blaze a trail to happy destiny.

Sincerely and Kindest Regards,

George Mentz, Esq.

References

Allen, J. (1998). *As You Think.* Edited with an introduction by M. Allen. Novato, CA: New World Library.

Aurelius, M. (1964) *Meditations.* M. Staniforth (trans.). London: Penguin.

The Bhagavad-Gita (1973) J. Mascaró (trans.). London: Penguin World's Classics.

Behrend, G. (1927) *Your Invisible Power.* Montana: Kessinger Publishing.

Carnegie, D. (1994). *How to Win Friends and Influence People.* New York: Pocket Books.

Carlson, R. (2001). *Don't Sweat the Small Stuff About Money.* New York, USA: Hyperion.

Chopra, D. (1996). *The Seven Spiritual Laws of Success.* London: Bantam Press.

Collier, R. (1970). *Be Rich.* Oak Harbor, Washington: Robert Collier Publishing.

Coelho, P. (1999). *The Alchemist.* Alan R. Clarke (trans.), London: HarperCollins.

Covey, S. R. (1989). *The 7 Habits of Highly Effective People.* London: Simon & Schuster.

Dyer, W. (1993). *Real Magic: Creating Miracles in Everyday Life.* New York: HarperCollins.

Eker, T. H. (2005). *Secrets of the Millionaire Mind: Mastering the Inner Game of Wealth.* New York: HarperCollins Publishers.

Emerson, R.W. (1993) *Self-Reliance.* Dover Publications.

Gawain, Shakti (1979). *Creative Visualization.* New World Library, Mill Valley USA.

Jordan, B. B. (2007). *The Laws of Thinking: 20 Secrets to Using the Divine Power of Your Mind to Manifest Prosperity.* Hay House and Bishop E. Bernard Jordan Books

Hill, N. (1960). *Think and Grow Rich.* New York: Fawcett Crest.

His Holiness the Dalai Lama, Cutler, H. C. (1999). *The Art of Happiness: A Handbook for Living.* London: Hodder & Stroughton.

James, W. (1902). *The Varieties of Religious Experience.* Longman Publishing, London, UK.

Jeffers, S. (1991) *Feel the Fear and Do It Anyway.* London: Arrow Books.

Lao-Tzu's Tao Te Ching (2000) T. Freke (trans.). Introduction by M. Palmer. London: Piatkus.

Maltz, M. (1960). *Psycho-Cybernetics.* New York: Pocket Books.

Marden, O. S. (1997). *Pushing to the Front, or Success under Difficulties, Vols. 1–2.* Santa Fe, California: Sun Books.

Mentz, C. W. H. (2007). *Masters of the Secrets: And the Science of Getting Rich and Master Key System Expanded: Bestseller Version.* Bloomington, Indiana, United States: Xlibris Corp.

Mentz, C. W. H. (2006). *How to Master Abundance and Prosperity—The Master Key System Decoded.* Bloomington Indiana: Xlibris Pub.

Mentz, C. W. H. (2005). *The Science of Growing Rich.* Bloomington, Indiana: Xlibris Publishing.

Mentz, G. S. *Other Books by Mentz.* http://www.lulu.com/gmentz

Mulford, P. (1908). *Thoughts Are Things: Essays Selected from the White Cross Library.* London: G. Bell and Sons, Ltd.

Murphy, J. (1963). *The Power of Your Subconscious Mind.* New Jersey: Prentice Hall.

Peale, N.V. (1996) *The Power of Positive Thinking,* New York: Ballantine Books.

Ponder, C. (1962). *The Dynamic Laws of Prosperity.* Camarillo, California: DeVorss & Co.

Price, J. R. (1987). *The Abundance Book.* Carlsbad, California: Hay House.

Roman, S., & Packer, D. R. (2008). Creating Money: *Attracting Abundance.* Tiburon, California: H. J. Kramer, Inc., published in a joint venture with New World Library.

Scovell Shinn, F. (1998) *The Game of Life and How to Play It,* Saffron Walden: C.W. Daniel.

Seicho-no Iye (生長の家). Books by Dr. Masaharu Taniguchi.

Smiles, S. (2002). *Self-Help: With Illustrations of Character, Conduct, and Perseverance.* Oxford: Oxford University Press.

Thoreau, H.D. (1986) *Walden and Civil Disobedience,* introduction by M. Meyer. New York: Penguin.

Tracy, B. (1993). *Maximum Achievement: Strategies and Skills That Will Unlock Your Hidden Powers to Succeed.* New York: Fireside.

Troward, T. (1904). *The Edinburgh Lectures on Mental Science.* New York: Dodd, Mead & Company.

Wattles, W. D. (1976). *Financial Success through the Power of Thought: The Science of Getting Rich.* Rochester, Vermont: Destiny Books.

Wilkinson, B. (2000). *The Prayer of Jabez.* Colorado Springs, CO USA, OR: Multnamah Publishers.

ABOUT THE AUTHOR

Dr. George Mentz JD MBA CILS - is an award-winning author, counselor of law, professor and premier, sought-after educator, revolutionary author, and global management consultant. Dr. Mentz is universally referenced by his clientele, friends, and colleagues as one of the most thoughtful, enthusiastic, and empathetic leaders in the business world today. Dr. Mentz is the founder of the GAFM Global Academy of Financial Management® and has published extensively in the fields of law, e-business, fiscal policy, taxation, finance, entrepreneurship, marketing, international wealth management, and success strategy.

Dr. Mentz has advised and consulted on success and education with the US government, United Nations, NGOs, foreign governments, and Fortune 500 companies while helping people from around the world improve their education and careers through education awards or scholarships.

Both on his own and through his companies, he has provided business training and VIP courses in over fifty countries worldwide. Dr. Mentz received his Doctor of

Jurisprudence (JD) and MBA degrees after attending legal and business coursework at Loyola University, Catholique University Campus Belgium, William and Mary Law School, & Tulane University while doing research and courses in Austria, Spain, Belgium, Mexico, and Brazil. Dr. Mentz is the first person in the United States to achieve "Quad Designation" Status as a JD, MBA, qualified/licensed financial planner and wealth manager, and Qualified/Certified Financial Consultant & Planner. Dr. Mentz is the recipient of national awards and honors for his contributions in the fields of management, excellence, teaching, charity, leadership, and public speaking. He even completed all of the International business and law courses related to foreign diplomacy that are typically recommended by the US State Department.

In recent years, George Mentz has been named an expert and leader for his publications and he has been honored by mainstream media as a brain trust member and part of the Dream Team of Financial Writers for mainstream media outlets. He has served on the advisory boards of many institutions, including the Global Finance Forum in Switzerland, Various FinTech Companies World E-

Commerce Forum in the UK, Certified Economist Association of Africa, China Wealth Management Institute of Hong Kong, Arab Academy - Standards Council, International Project Management Commission, a US medical training school, international masters programs, a law school's graduate program, and various charities.

Dr. Mentz is an IBA award winning author, NewsMax Columnist, and two-time national award-winning professor who has been a contributor and expert for various organizations. Some of Dr. Mentz's bestselling books and publications include: Quantum Bliss, The Illuminati Handbook, *CWM Chartered Wealth Manager Guide*, *Project Manager Executive Guide*, internet college recruiting and marketing materials, the *Wealth Management Executive Guide*, *Online Credibility in the Finance World – Protecting Your Web Reputation & Company Brand*, *The Secret Powers of Highly Effective People*, *Spiritual Wealth Management*, *Wealth Management and Financial Planning*, and many more. Published in many journals, Dr. Mentz is a pioneer in the movements of GECC global executive certification training, international wealth management, internet marketing, and human potential.

Dr. Mentz and his executive development companies have been featured, presented, or quoted in the *NASDAQ News, Forbes, Reuters, Morningstar, Yahoo Finance, Wall Street Globe, The Hindu National, El Norte Latin America*, the *Financial Times, NYSSA New York Securities Analysts News, The China Daily, The Department of Education ERIC Library,* US Department of Labor brochures, *Black Enterprise, The San Francisco Chronicle, Associated Press*, and the *Arab Times.*

You can contact Dr. Mentz at his website, www.gmentz.com

This work is mostly original works created from analyzing the philosophy of the great teachers of the past, and the creative revision, original insights, revised or updated public domain works, or the enhancement of the philosophy of great gurus to deliver the universal truth, secrets of prosperity and peace of mind.

Made in the USA
Las Vegas, NV
20 March 2024

87465957R00069